Ascension Flight 999

The Last Call

Cheryl Lunar Wind & Friends

Ascension Flight 999

The Last Call

Some of the poems in this collection first appeared in We Are One, Follow the White Rabbit, Step Into New Earth and Illuminations From the Source chapbooks, on facebook.

Cover photo credit to Gary Eagle, 2025
Cover design credit to Rene Moraida, 2025

First edition.

Published by Alexander Agency Books,
Mount Shasta, California 96067

ISBN 979-8-9988971-3-9

Ascension Flight 999

The Last Call

Dedicated to Catherine Preus (8/28/1952-8/30/2025)
and Natalya Koogler (3/25/1958-9/9/2025)
and all those preceding us, with love.

Calling in Courage, Compassion
and Kindness for Humanity.
Calling in Discernment, Fortitude,
and Wisdom for all of us as we
face into these times.

The divisions we are taught to
perceive toward and about each other
are not the Truth of who we are.

Humanity is One Tribe with
many beautiful faces.
One Tribe together flowing
through times and seasons.

Flowing forth from The One
Original Source of All that Is.
Each one of us, an important
member of this Human Family.

Each one of us, a Fleck
of Eternal and Infinite.
Love, Natalya Koogler

**Ascension Flight 999
The Last Call**

Our choices now are---
to leave physically or do the inner work
upgrading our bodies for a very physical ascension.

This collection shares what this process feels like from
our fellow humans going through these intense times
and ways to succeed with ease and grace.

It is open and raw, expressing deep feelings and revelations.

Many thanks to all contributors, to Gary Eagle for cover photo and
Rene Moraida for cover design.

I'm in these final moments of summer,
slipping between the worlds of light and dark--
I AM part of every ceremony & every celebration.
I AM Life in ALL cycles.
I AM Love.
Blessed Be,
--- J. Shima Moore

I am there--A' Marie B. Thomas -Brown

"The movie plays the same whether it's the first time or the 99th
time", Indeed.

There is nothing new under the Sun, all is one and we to add our
records, "our tea" to the Akashic storehouse and teapot.

Great opportunity that you expressed here from your own
storehouse within the space of all that is (regarding poem *In-
Crowd*).

I am there. I've been here before and if life cedes on, will so again.
What am I eating and drinking, and what will be the sustenance of
my life story? I have the story and movie, now I'm working on the t-
shirt, 3-in-one!

I'm done.
And again, thank you.

Contents

Author and Contributor's pages

Freedom's Call
by Agatea

The last call for freedom rang--
faintly from deep within each heart.
The last call for freedom rang--

I don't know in this lifetime
the storms forgotten
that swept one after another
on this earth, over a century..
As wave followed wave
of Revolution.

The wind picked up a crumpled paper,
It was the poem of the soul
Silver and grey clouds came
and covered the Sun
Thunder cracked and lightning
struck the paper
disintegrating it.

I stood shocked as I watched
the poem disappear
Only ashes blown away
in different directions
by the wind.

Ashes to ashes and dust to dust
A Nation has fallen
But the People are standing
Freedom will choose from
the light within each heart
what they will stand for and
what the will create.

Storm clouds, quantum bird's eye view
by Zarah Chelsie Nicole Wolivar

As the storm clouds protect the skies from solar flares, a stranger appears in the field of flowers. Each flower representing different cultural races of humans and other beings.

The stranger looks at the Earth in a quantum bird's eye view, noticing the pandemonium that is building up. The stranger calls in the storms for balance to calm the chaos on Earth. Thunder hits during an eclipse. Lightning comes out of the shadow figure's finger tips spitting out light codes into the Earth.

For the Earth is a living being of light, as the Mother crystal in the center of the Earth is her heart and brain. She begs the shadow for help. The shadow figure promises the crystal Earth to help.

Because of the promise made the shadow figure fears death but knows it's only the beginning of life. The shadow's Inner being within activates. A peaceful presence spurs out of the shadow's body. It starts to rain heavily for a whole month putting out all chaotic fires that are not natural around the world.

The code activation within is combined to everything that lives. The words for the activation are "Change the old ways of the rules to the new ways, change the false prophesies and change the future". Silence the time travelers for they are naive. They do not choose our fate!

The stranger in the field knows that all we need is faith in each other.

The laws of the Universe allow us to choose our fate.

Break the reincarnation cycle.
We have ovaries for a reason.
Women are the portals to peace.

Cataclysmic Creation
by Cheryl

This explosive event is not the end all.
Earth shakes, quakes--

Woe, when mice weep.
Wink at the coming of the end of time.

Dine on your fear--
chew it up
spit it out.

Take it in stride--
Keep riding.
Be a 'Low Rider'.
Ride out the storm--
Big Bang.
'*Riders of the Storm*'
Thunderbirds.

Soar Free
like a flame--
Be the fire.

Lead.
Leaders lead.
Leaders of the pack.

Building An Ark
by Cheryl

Like Noah's Ark,
we can survive the flood.

The Nephilim have created
too much mischief--
we will have to go somewhere else,
or become something new--

The becoming.
Metamorphosis.

Can we survive
the flipping of the poles--
like 'cow tipping' on farms
by mischievous humans.

Who's turning Earth's axis?
Giants? Titans? Unseen forces?

We're at the end of this world;
not cataclysmic--
more like Evolution.

Many Waters--Wells of Water
to Navigate.

Retreat, until it is safe to come out.
You alone can save yourself.

I am building my own Ark.

How will the journey change us?
Metamorphosis.

Soul
by Cheryl

See that little black spot by the sun today?

It's my soul out there,
Searching for a way home.

I am a dove---cast out
of Noah's Ark.

Hunting
for a branch of my own.

Jumbled feelings and memories
glide by--
briefly--
not long enough--
to get--
a foothold.

Same old thing as yesterday.

The impermanence of it all.

My mind is a sentry--
guards against,
lies, traps, and endless detours.

My soul longs for home.

Stranger in a Strange Land
by Cheryl

She's in a strange place.

Strange & difficult times--
(times of transition)

Pink Floyd's
wall of flamingoes...

Truth is Stranger than fiction.

Fill it...Filled...Full
Full on...Face it...

Face it Full on.

Holiday. Take it, Make it, Break it.
Break out--dance

Snap, Clap---Hold onto your hat--
Because it's about to get real.

"There's a little black spot on the sun today,
It's my soul out there."
What is she doing out there?
Come back here, we're not done yet.

Patience my dear.

Turmoil Laments
by Mercy Talley

I look at my feet ~

Creator gave me these feet
to walk the path of Truth

I choose Truth road
to guide me thru
chaos swirls
& conniving distractions

clarity provides my Soul
fresh air breathing
with strength

no siphoning of
vital life energy
when seeing
thru deception

aware of my feet
on sweet Appalachian soil
heart songs
erupt out of
turmoil laments ~

~~~

The sound hum
of breath & blood flow
rivers of life force thru veins
coursing melodies in mind waves
soaring soft spoken upon pages
longing to land wistfully
beckoning bright
discovery
dancing
into
dawn
~

The Sun Sends Light
by Shivrael

A tapestry of light codes
is being woven by your higher self
right now, in this moment.
I see the strands light up!

My Soul's fractal
created this part-can you see it?
Reality weaving
the beauty of a rainbow
with everyone's unique frequency.

This is how the light gets in
through the fiber optic strands
of our being and of creation.
Soul expresses
from our mind's eyes
into matter.

We are the manifesters-
Manifesting a new era
based on love,
founded in co-operation
"Collaboration" is the tagline of divine.

Messages sent are to remind us how to
co-create Heaven on Earth.
We can do it!

Galactic Breakfast Joint
by Shivrael

When the cosmic egg
was cracked open,
a galaxy landed in
the frying pan of divine
and a new world was born.

"How do you like your eggs?
She asked-
The Divine Mother is
playing the part of a waitress.

"Why sunny side up
with a side of miracles."

"That's how we roll" she replies
and hands the order to the short order cook,
disguised as God.

They are always serving up
new miracles
when we pray.

The Divine has the best restaurant
at the end of the galaxy.

Return to Kindness
by Jane Seeley

At the lake with the passing clouds
I see myself what choice I have
to do no harm
And return to kindness
That's how the light gets in

To understand compassion
manifest in all my actions
to do no harm
And return to kindness

It starts with thoughts that start in me,
changing my reality
to do no harm
And return to kindness

A gift is given each breath I take
as I begin to ruminate
to do no harm
And return to kindness

A leaf, a breeze, a thought, a sneeze,
an everlasting eternity
to do no harm
And return to kindness
That's how the light gets in.

~~~

The crescent moon
Rosh Hashanah ends
And yet another year begins.
May happy peace fill all your days
And all the love surround you
Forgive be free
Just let it be
And see the stars around you
~

Perceptions of Peace and Kindness

by Cathleen Alexander

According to the Law of Perception,

Beauty is in the eye of the beholder.

I choose to behold beauty.

I choose to behold peace.

I choose to hold the Peaceful Presence.

How many eyes see Presence?

How many eyes see Peace?

How many say "AYE" to peace?

You are the apple of my eye, my "I."

I see you in my mind's eye, even before we've met.

My mind chooses to let the Light and levity in.

The light shines.

I behold peace.

I perceive a world of people returning to kindness.

Have we not been kind before?

Let me return each act of kindness by being a kind giver myself.

How have I given kindness today?

Let me count the ways.

Let me count on the Way.

The way is peace,

returning to kindness,

beholding the Beautiful Peaceful Presence within.

I see how the Light gets in ---

11   Through the cracks, Through new perceptions.

You can do this hard thing
by Cheryl

We are at the close of a cosmic cycle.
Bring your peaceful presence
to the cycles of pandemonium.

Forget the storms that cause you pain.
I don't know the storms forgotten.

Find your Balance.
Flamingoes shift perspective.

Listen to your inner voice--
Universal Law of Perception.

It takes courage and discrimination--
But
You can do this hard thing.

The eclipse graces our reality--
Cracking the cosmic egg,
letting light in.

Twist your mind's eye--
Break the shell of control
and
Open up to mysterious humility.

You can do this hard thing.

The last call
(A message about change and fear of change)
by Timothy Hershelman

Late night, order with a twist,
don't discriminate or put on bravado.

Have some humility and grace, because
the euphoria is like a passing eclipse.
You can always close the cycle,
but what kind of pandemonium would that be...?

Hope Lives Inside You
Pradeep Nawarathna

May each morning bring a fresh breath of hope,
filling your heart with new energy.

Let your inner light shine brighter than any worry,
showing you the way forward.

Feel the quiet strength inside you—
it's proof of your resilience and your ability to feel joy.

Whatever challenges come your way, trust in yourself.
You're capable of turning obstacles into growth.

Let gratitude guide your day,
helping you notice the many blessings around you.

Release yesterday's weight.
Each step you take is supported by love,
leading you toward peace and purpose.

Find comfort in life's simple gifts—
a kind word, a smile, the beauty of nature.
Let them nourish your soul.

Keep your mind clear, your heart open, and your spirit lifted.
A beautiful future is waiting.
Every new beginning holds promise.

Hope lives inside you—
it's strong, steady, and ready to lead you home.

Return to Kindness
by Cheryl

They say:
Truth is Stranger than Fiction.

It's enough to delay my Bravado--

Dreams of cumulus clouds bring euphoria.

How does the light get in?
You can do this hard thing.

I don't know the storms forgotten.

It's the Last Call to
Return to Kindness.

You can do this hard thing!

Prayer
by Shambala

Teach Us to Pray. Prayer is Power. Prayer is Communion.
Through Prayer we arrive at the Zero Point
~ The Fount of All Truth ~
The Return to Source.
In this everything is reborn, everything made new.

Prayer is the Doorway to Miracles.
We see all of creation with eyes made new and innocent.
Prayer brings us into a secret place and then our prayers are
answered.

Our Prayers are a circle.
As We pray them, they begin to return to us.
Some in circles of breath ~ Some in a circle of an aeon.

One Prayer is Letting It Go and Letting It Be.
Prayer is dynamically creating reality. It is a way of reaching
the deepest inner sanctum to hear the voice of the absolute.
Prayer is moving into realization activation.
So Please, take time to pray.
Pray and let your whole being fill with light and marvel at the
Magnificence.

Let Gratitude and Thanksgiving fill our Prayers.
May we remember to show our thanks in many ways for all we
have received.

O' MA' TAKUYASI

Let It All Go
by Shambala

Leave it all behind.

Every moment is the Anniversary of Something in the
great Web of Life.
In this moment,
I find myself in the Meadow wih the insects and the flowers,
wondering if I will ever fulfill a higher destiny or if I'll just chase
mirages and run from myself forever.

We are like the flowers
~ Bloom for a moment, the Season ~
then pass away.
If I collected all of the tears ever shed,
would they fill up a crater lake?

Let it all go and behold with the Inner Eye,
the eye that scales the heights to stand where
The Saints Are Marching In.
On each banner is written the
~ Words of Life ~ Statements of Truth ~ Declarations of Victory.

There is a Golden Radiance Upon Everything.

Vajra Guru Padme Siddhi Hum

Late Night Revelations
by Cheryl

One door closes---
another one opens.

Completion
Closing
Last call---

Time to shift perspective---

There is a crack in the cosmic egg--
light code activations
stream in--

I don't know from where.

It's Pandemonium--
anymore--

The Last Call
by Maya Rawitch

Don't drink the Koolaid--
it's how the light gets in.

Peek at its shimmering, glistening surface
reflecting eudaimonia.

Where else would it shine but on the cosmic egg?
The light beams crack the egg with thundering bravado.
Mind's eye twists to reveal life's pandemonium.

Gracious, yet tired--
I don't know the storms forgotten.
Light code activation.
Faith has shaken.

All is brazen in the lunar eclipse.
Mayhem drifts--
her cold shoulders touch mine, prompting endless bliss.
Closing cycles.
Breaking bread, baking from the forming egg.
Crack in the cosmic egg builds Easter energy.

Don't drink the koolaid.
Collect your bravado.
Let it accumulate in cumulus clouds overhead.

You can do this hard thing.

Let the cumulonimbus bring condensation to life--
at the dimly lit light for grace to appear once again;
in our life, in the late night--tightly wrapped in delight,
faceless as one in the mind's eye might be
left invisible,
hence the light goes bright at the sight
of the last call of night.

Birthday Thoughts
by Susan Redwine

Personally,
I Celebrate My Birthday Every Day of the Year!
I never Understood that One Day Deal
In Earth Years I Am 66 Today and
I am Loving Every Minute of it!
Even the Challenges, which stem mostly
From Myself
Ok ...All of Myself!

Although I Am Celebrating My Earth Years here, today,
now on this Planet, since going Home and returning,
I Have Remembered and Know that
At this SAME Time being physically 66,
I AM a Divine and Eternal Being and Soul.
Earth Years do not Define Me.

I Always look back on the Woman I was last year and
See and Feel how Far I've Come.
One of My Biggest Life Challenges, this
lifetime was Staying on this Planet!
Because I have had 'Trips' back Home
(Heaven, Paradise, No human word can adequately describe 'IT')
Staying On the Earth and Making the Commitment
To Be Going BIG before returning Home,
Bringing Heaven to Earth as Best I Can,
I have Committed to Stay Unwavering
in My Peace, Understanding and Joy.
With the Knowing Although We Never Die,
Our Earth Time IS Limited.
And When I Do Look Back,
I Want to See that I Took NOTHING for Granted.
Each and Every Moment Was and IS a Gift
that I gave and give to Myself.

My Birthday Message From Me
to You is...
To Honor Each Other
To Cherish ALL of Our Earthly Moments!
To REMEMBER Your Divine Greatness
And the POWER of OUR LOVE.

Forgive Yourself and then Each Other,
NO Blame and NO Shame.
NO Judgments.
Express Your Love Freely and Come From THAT Place of Love.
Over and Over and Over Again.
Until Everyone Can Hear and Feel the Message
Of Unconditional Love.
On Earth..As it IS in Heaven.

Remember Each and Every Day that
YoU are the Gift to This Planet!
I AM Beyond Grateful to have had the
Opportunity and the Honor to Meet
and Connect with So Many Amazing and
Beautiful Souls around the World
Please Know that this Has Been One of
My Biggest GiFTS!
Thank You for Being a Part of My Earth
Journey and Allowing Me to Be a Part of Yours
Today and Everyday I Am Celebrating the Fact
That I Made it This Far!
I Can't Wait to See What Happens Next.

More...
by Janine Savient

Within the warmth of my being
I touch the softness of soul
Loving what I'm feeling
I open more to know

Inward ... always inward
Curiously feeling my way
Gently moving, softly flowing
I'm home in love's sway

Inward, there is beauty
In the depth, I will find
All I've ever searched for
no longer am I blind

My heart encourages me
deeper through its door
My longing, softly calls me
yes, more more...

I dance and I play
within hearts pure desires
Melding Into beauty
of passions deep fires

In the depth of my fullness
and power, I soar
In body, embodied
I feel the roar, for more

Beauty always rising
heart having its say
Strength found in softness
now is my way

It's all about love
Internal at first
Then filling this world
Love quenching the thirst

Hush beloveds
Hear your hearts call
Beauty - awaits you
Feel it's deep pull

The day has come
the moment has arrived
when, through loves presence
we feel more fully alive

Seven Virtues Dancing
Elizabeth Carrillo

Upon the floor, a sacred space, a stage,
Seven virtues, turning life's new page.
The music starts... a whisper and a beat,
And virtue finds its rhythm for the feet.

The first is *Humility*, a silent grace,
Who lowers the eyes and finds their proper place.
Her dance begins not with a bold advance,
But in the pause, the step of circumstance.
She bows to all, the simple and the great,
And finds in every partner her true state.

Then *Chastity*, in flowing and modest gown,
Whose movements are a promise for the crown.
She turns and glides with purity and light,
A self-controlled and focused, quiet might.
Her spirit finds its freedom not in lust,
But in a higher and a holier trust.

Kindness, with open arms, invites the lost,
To join the circle, counting not the cost.
Her gentle spin, a gesture to the soul,
To make the lonely and the broken whole.
She steps with empathy and tender care,
A dance of fellowship beyond compare.

Patience takes her turn, with measured sway,
And knows the dance will lengthen through the day.
She waits for hurried partners to find their pace,
And holds her balance with enduring grace.
She does not rush, but trusts the coming rhyme,
And finds the perfect tempo in due time.

Next, *Temperance*, with every steady stride,
Knows how to find the path and be a guide.
She does not rush, but moves with conscious thought,
And finds a peaceful rhythm, dearly sought.
No fevered spinning, lost within the throng,
But balanced measure to the perfect song.

Diligence enters with a focused step,
A tireless motion, holding to the prep.
He trains his feet to follow every beat,
And makes the difficult appear so sweet.
He spins and leaps with ever-growing skill,
His persistence proving the iron of his will.

And last, comes *Charity*, whose dance is love,
A selfless motion from the heavens above.
She takes the lead, but only to release,
And gives her all to bring the dancers peace.
She is the music and the dance's soul,
And with her, every scattered part is whole.

And so the virtues dance, a living chain,
Across the floor, through pleasure and through pain.
Each step a choice, each gesture is a sign,
That in the movement, all can be divine.

I know I will be fine
Bodhi Holum Johnson

As an alchemist I resist
To follow anything that focus drifts
I take their emotions
I swirl them with loving motion
I spin it wide with intention
I stay focused... invention
No fear no spilt emotions as I use the electricity
To reciprocate my vision... my dream
It's going to get worse they say
Still I smile whilst I play
Electric clay
I give conscious gratitude
To all the fake stories and fake news
I know I will be fine
As the now breathes the divine
To calm the mind and let soul speak
To never let our spirit get weak
No divide...... just unity
I can cook garden and clean
We can bring our ingredients in this dream
Remember that when triggers are triggering

At Home In Myself
Trudie Giordano

This last eclipse in my sign....closing cycles
No longer a stranger in a strange land

At home in myself

Discovering eudaimonia --
the euphoria of achieving this lifelong goal!
The storms forgotten...the perspective shift
The grace, humility, gratitude...
The peaceful presence.

It took courage and a steady gaze in the mind's eye.
You can end delay and do this hard thing…
that's how the light gets in.
And brings a return to kindness.

Art of Exiting
by Molesley Bridgette author of The Queen Code

Exiting is an art.
You do not have to burn bridges to walk away.
You can leave with grace, dignity, and foresight.
Staying in what drains you is a form of self-abandonment.
Plan your exits. Do them quietly. Do them cleanly.
Exiting without drama preserves your energy for the next season.

Art of Trusting Yourself
by Le'Vell Zimmerman

"Doing this" because another person "is doing that"
is to operate as "a follower".

Leaders act from their own intuitive guidance beyond
being manipulated or "reactive" here within this hologram.

Trusting yourself is an artform beloved.

The more in touch you are with how you feel, the more
graceful your own decision making as a Soul.

11:11

In-Crowd
by Cheryl

You say you want your freedom.
"Who am I to keep you down?"
(Don't want to commit, that's ok)

Like a moth to flame---
always drawn to the brightest light--
seeking, wanting more.

Always needing to be in the In-Crowd--
the more buzz
the better---

Oh--that's the happening thing
I gotta be there--
You don't realize it's happening
wherever YOU are.
Do you think only the Top 100 will ascend?
It's not a contest.
We are All worthy.

So love the part of yourself
that's always striving
to be 'on top'---
to succeed---
It's counterproductive.
Isn't it tiring?

I was there.
I'm cool.
I went to that party.

The movie plays the same whether
it's the first time or the 99th---

Looking back on our lives---
Endings & Beginnings
What's your legacy look like?
What records are you making for
the Akashic Story Board?
They last forever. Think about it.

A Visitor in the Guest House that Welcomes All
by Shivrael

Anger shoved her foot
in the door
So I let her in,
and held space for her.

First, she threw some dishes
breaking them.
Well, we didn't need those plates anyway.

Then she helped me beat some rugs.

I explained that
when you are feeling emotional
It is a good time to make art.
I gave her some thick crayons
for her inner child.
She made me some pictures
with lots of red.

Anger was becoming more mindful
but still had to find expression.
She whispered her secret
revenge fantasies
So I gave her a paper and a pen.
She wrote a poem
to express and process all the rage,
anger, and hurt she carried.

At this point, she needed to cry
and I held her sobbing
until it was done.

Then she borrowed my teddy bear
and went to sleep.

I guess this is how to put
Anger to bed?
Let her have free rein,
then show her that she can channel it.
Let her speak it and listen.

30

Let the flow of it run out of her
in red rivers of expression-
every nuance of emotion felt
until she can rest easy
and be at peace.

Human Life
by Daniel Stone

How to move from the head
To the heart;
How to open to your soul that is waiting for the moment
When your body will receive
without resistance
Arrive finally
To experience this human
Life.

Tuning In
by Shivrael

Allow the codes to unlock.
999.
Ending, new beginning
Are one.
Follow the breadcrumbs
Of your soul

Go within.
Fine tune your frequency.
Dial in your
soul's signal.

Trick or Treat
by Cheryl

Heya--
         Got any tricks?
Can you pull a rabbit out of your hat?
         I can!

My pink backpack
is endless
and weightless...

It carries all my lessons, guides and gifts.

Like a magic tophat--
In it....

You'll find a rabbit
who only eats Trix
bright pink flamingoes
and
the lessons of a lifetime.

Heart Stands Still
by Rune Darling, Satarah Erikke Ingvild

The current Rune
Roasted in Blood
.

Carefully Put Your Foot
In the stone
.

The hand of water
Tying the 7 chakras in ties
.

Eternal Energy Manifesto
The Euclidean Space in Mol*
.

Capability to Comprehension
When You Speak From The Heart
.

Responsibility awakens in the space of the heart
The Ego Rests And Remains Eternally Silent
.

The HeartBlood Is Flowing
When You Invite Your Soul
.

The Point of Now in the Heart Stands Still
Opening Up and Time Passing
.

Give yourself the Opportunity
Awakening the Love of the Heart
.

*Mol--In Danish, the word 'mol' means moth.
The band Mol chose this name to reflect their music,
symbolizing duality, beauty and transformation.

Love is the answer
by Rune Darling

We Will Come To Life
In A Blink Of Gods Eye
.

Let go and just be free
WE WILL love you unconditionally
.

Come just as you are
Don't need apologies
.

Know that you are worthy
I AM Down on My Knees
I'll take your bad days with your good
Walk through the storm, I would

I do it all because I LOVE YOU
.

Unconditional, unconditionally
We Will love you unconditionally
.

There is no fear now
Let go and just be free
I will love you unconditionally
.

So open up your heart and just let it begin
Open up your heart and just let it begin
Open up your heart
.

Acceptance is the key to be
To be truly free
.

Will You Do the Same For Me?
Unconditional, unconditionally
.

We Are
Forever
Changing
.

Pioneers
by Susan Redwine

We are here at this Amazing Time on Earth,
In this Ascending Dimension of Challenges and Hardships
to Birth a New Earth and Reality.

A Reality of Higher Light,
of Higher Consciousness,
of Higher Potentiality,
of Unity and Compassion.
Thus,
Bringing Earth to Heaven and Heaven to Earth.

We have Volunteered and have Incarnated in the Physical
to Aide in Liberating others To their True Power and Light.
To their Innate Knowledge and Sovereignty.
To Remind Everyone to Love each Other
and ALL Beings Freely and without Conditions or Judgment.
As IT is in the Higher Dimensions.

We are Pioneers in this Ascension Process.
We are Reality Creators and Earth Energy Transmuters,
Alchemists, Healers and Game Changers.

We have Come--
To Open Hearts
To Open Souls
To Open Minds
To Our Higher Knowing.
To the Truth of Our Divine Beings.
To the Understanding of Our Now place
in this Vast Multi-verse of Love and Light.

We have come to Banish the lower toxic energies from the
Hearts and Minds of those Who are Experiencing symptoms:
fear, grief, loneliness, or anything holding one back from
Remembering Who they Authentically Are.

We have Chosen to be here on this Amazing Earth, to aide
in Integrating Shadows and Transforming Fear into Love.
Bringing Unity, Peace, and Harmony

Throughout the Galaxies,
The Multiverses,
The Planets.
Throughout Time Eternally.

We have come to Remind Others
Of the Inter-connectedness of ALL Souls
and Sentient Beings.
That there is NO Separation.
That what We Do to each Other,
We Do To Ourselves.
To Remember in All of Sacred Earth Moments,
That All Beings Share the Same Divine Essence,
We are ALL Energetically Connected.
We are ALL ONE Family.

When Your Ascending
(Written to the melody *When Your Smiling*)
by Alex Hogstrum

When you're as-cending, when your as-cending the new world opens to you

When you let your loving heart shine you lift up everyone too

But when you're thinking   thoughts that are dark

You fall back down and make a world that is stark

So keep as-cending, 'cause when you're as-cending

The whole world as-cends with you

When you rise up to higher dim-ensions you only see what is true

Separation will vanish, leaving only love and me and you

But if you choose to see light and dark

The union you feel will soon fall a-part

So keep as-cending, 'cause when your as-cending,

You bring up everyone with you!

Ode to Divine Timing
by Shivrael

We are all just dancing through life
making it up as we go.
This cosmic improvisation
seems random upon the surface
yet underneath, it is divine.

How do I run into soul family
at the exact moment
I arrive at the park?
What a blessing this is!
How does divine timing work
to synchronize us all
so we meet and share our
medicine with one another?

We are here to walk each other home,
to bring wholeness and unconditional love
and to heal and open hearts.

I love it that my inward journey
is reflected back in the grand design-
appreciating how puzzle pieces
find one another.
It happens through people and opportunities
but it is really grace.

All divinely synchronized
like a planetary sized ballroom
full of dancers meeting one another
again and again,
coming full circle
because of grace.

Garment of Ascension
by Shambala

A Gentle Breeze ~ Soft waves lapping on the shore ~
Sunlight filtering thru leaves that rustle in the wind.
Sunrays refracting on the water ~
This is the Garment of Ascension.
Sunrays piercing the Kaleidoscope of our eyes.
This is a Holy Transmission.
Golden white light bathing us ~ This is the baptism.

It feels like a summer evening in a thousand different places on the
earth. This so we can anchor the column of light.

The Glorious White Light is--
Healing us, Empowering us.
Filling us with:
the Consciousness of Christ
the Gumption of Saint Germaine
the Royalty of Rumi
the Happiness of Hafiz
the Wonder of Whitman
the Sonnets of Shakespeare
the Riches of Rockefeller.

This Light is filling us with:
the Peace of the Param Guru
the Praise of David on his harp
the Intimate Inspirations of Saint Theresa.

This Golden Light connects us into the network of
The Great White Brotherhood ~
A Quantum Mind field of unlimited possibilities quickening within
us our own sacred blueprint of unique expressions and service.

We bask in the meditation of the mystics and our hearts are
comforted with kindness and caring. The Golden Diamond Light
contains all the Holy Teachings in an elixir of amrita that pours thru
us, satisfying the deepest longings of our heart. These are the
gentle waves rolling at our feet from the Great Central Sun. The
Lord of Host's blessings are in this Light.

And So It Is ~ Hosanna in the Highest

Color Therapy
by Cheryl

I have a pair of knickers---
pink, blue and white checked.
The colors are perfect.
The blue is a true blue---
like a cornflower and dark water.
The pink is a carnation.
The white is the mediator
between the two.

I am wearing the balance of
power and love
of masculine and feminine.

Rays of color
are here
for our healing.
Assisting
our return
to source.

Like the Antakarana---Rainbow Bridge.
We can shut our eyes and go there.
Fly---
like pink and blue birds.
Time to fly on---
Join our fellows--
Masters.
Move on to the next place--

"On the road again....many more miles
On the road again."
It has not been a failed mission---The work has been accomplished.

I feel sadness
at leaving.
What's for me now?
I am promised
it will be good.
That First Big Step
the historic moon walk.

41

The Final Song
by Cheryl

Say yes to music.

Chant, Drum, Dance.
Chant the words that you know.
You carry the song in your hearts.
Connect with the original beat.

Do you hear the cosmic tone?
The Bell is ringing.
Join the Universal Ohm.

Become Free.
Know Yourself.
Share your freedom.

Carry that feeling where ever you go.
Hear the final tune.
Be a clear vessel
and
Radiate the song
of
Love, Light and Peace.

There is a calling.
A Last call.
The Final Song.

The Final song is playing.
Listen.
The birds are singing
the Final Song.
One last chance---
to make a stand.

Stand up for right.
Be a protector---
        of the children, of the animals,
        of all Earth's inhabitants.
Be a guardian.

Stretch out your hand---
help a brother in need. *

Use your energy
to bless all life.
Pay it forward.
Pay with your Ka.
Live. Love. Give.

*Let's dance
one last dance.
It's the last dance,
last dance for love.* *

* Bill Withers, Lean on Me, 1972.
* Donna Summer, Last Dance, 1978.

Eudaimonia
by Phillip Ortiz

The summoning of summer's end;
Fallen fruit begs for rain.
Cumulus clouds crown the Western Peaks.

Advancing like chess pieces, rising, twisting,
overtaking the soft flute of the finch
with the Howling of Wind's mysterious Mystery.

They build their dark temples with bravado,
resolutely eclipsing what was warm & bright,
activating the encoded light.

And They Whisper
by Kazi Ayaz Mahesar

We were never seeking land
Nor peace that ends at borders
We were listening
To a hush older than wind
A pull softer than fate

They called us wanderers
But we were only walking
Toward what remembered us
We had no map in our hands
Only a sign written in light

We are the road that wasn't drawn
The shard that didn't shatter
The name before it was forgotten

Once, we broke
And the breaking became music
Once, we wept
And the tear became a river
A river that flowed against time

You may know now
We were not lost
We are returning
We are the void that walks
Until it becomes a door

And when you see the moon tonight
Look closely
You will find her following
Something, only you remember

The same stars
We are seeing together!

45

Caravan
by Kazi Ayaz Mahesar

Renewal of Pledge of Allegiance - - -

Renewal of the covenant of faithfulness is no one.
If the soul is moving, there is no caravan.

Is it a wide orbit or a horror idea?
It is every time, so there is no one in the end.

Every drop speaks, every breath sobs.
She says something happened, no one is dumb here.

If you listen, it listens to whatever river flows.
If you look, it hurts, if you don't look, there is no one kind.

Sometimes the boat also looks like Noah.
When there is no earth, there is no sky.

Renewal of the covenant of faithfulness is no one.
If there is a caravan, there is no one to go with the soul.

There is no caravan by Cheryl
with credit given to Kazi Ayaz Mahesar
for inspiration and words in quotes

Who do you pledge your allegiance to?
"Every time--there is no one in the end."

Is there anyone kind left?

Why renew the covenant?
Are we all dumb here?

Don't look for kindness,
because it hurts too much.

We are dropping our robes,
like flies,
dropping.

Where are the faithful?
Only the trees.
Don't cut them down,
they are survival.

Make an Ark out of human flesh--
Is it lasting--the covenant?

We destroy the earth, we destroy
ourselves.

How will our souls travel?
"It is every time, so there is no one in the end."

What happened to her?
Who to blame.
What to understand?
Why keep trying?

"Every drop speaks, every breath sobs."
Listen to your own river flowing.

My soul wants to move---
call a taxi--"there is no caravan"
47

Are we all in denial?
Why renew the covenant
of the faithful,
"there is no one"

"When there is no earth, there is no sky"
then we are free.

Heal the Illusion
by Le'Vell Zimmerman

All of Earth Humanities collective on many levels have "grievances" beloved...

However, you have to start with you.

Feeling that you can't heal until collective injustices are reconciled is to
keep yourself dependent on this external holographic illusion.

When you heal, the illusion will heal.

Being that you are the foundation of eternity,
only you can bring about change.

Your anger, resentment, bitterness, judgment, and sadness is only fueling the continuation of that which you say you don't prefer.

When you change, the world you observe will change.

The responsibility is yours beloved.

In truth, Earth Humanity is presently "waiting on you"...

You are The Leaders here.

Truly awakened Souls are not "waiting on" anything or anyone.

Leaders go first.

All were chosen...

Only a few responded.

-Command Team

Self Care
by Le'Vell Zimmerman

You have to take care of yourself if you intend to continue supporting others more beloved.

Self Love is the foundation of All Love.

When you live to serve all Life, Self care is "vital".

We "practice what we preach" here.

-333

This is "not a race" beloved...

It's a marathon.

Taking care of yourself is necessary to keep going.

Masters know this.

-333

Today
by Dave Harvey

Today I will see love where I have not seen love
before.
Today I will see magic where I have not seen
magic before.
Today I will see unity where I have not seen unity
before.
Today I will see peace where I have not seen
peace before.
Today I will see opportunity where I have not seen
opportunity before.
Today I will see appreciation where I have not seen
appreciation before.
Today I will see beauty where I have not seen
beauty before.
Today

The End Game
by Rune Darling

In This World
Dimensional Doors
Are Frequencies
.

In The Power Of Now
We Enter The Doors Between
We Are Entering The End Game
.

Surrendering It All Is Key
Breaking Bad Habits
Of An Unbalanced Ego
.

Cracked Open The Egg
Birthing The Divine
Feminine & Masculine
.

As We Run Out Of Time
Christ Consciousness
Is Upon Us For Evermore
.

Delivering Hope
In The Quantum Field
In A HeartBeat

This Is The Day
by Shambala

The Prophecy Of Love
This Is The Day
We Receive The White Dove
This Is The Day All Earth Is Bathed In White Fire
This Is The Day
The Children Lead Us Home

Prophecy Of Love
Hearalded By The Winds
Sung By The Mountains
Announced By The Angels
Carried By The Streams
Delivered By The Masters

Prophecy Of Love
This Is The Day
Prophecy Of Love
Come This Way
Into The Land Of Milk And Honey
Into The Land Of Joy and Peace
Into The Life
Of Love For Each Other

Destiny Revisited
by J. Shima Moore

Eternally
dancing from star to star,
cycle to cycle,
peeling back layers of social niceties
and expectation,
using occult knowledge to pierce veils

Multitudes of shiny illusions
promoted by the Matrix,
ever distracting,
ceaselessly sucking us in
and spitting us out,
derailing us from seeking Life's true purpose
and more importantly,
the purpose of *our* Life.

Stop-the-world-I-want-to get-off moments
barely remembered, lurk in the dark
long ago feelings, lingering ghosts--back East,
turning a particular corner
on the way home.

For years the Dark~
scared the bejesus out of me
sunshine and roses helped overcome the Void,
learning to pretend,
to "act as if".

Even so, until diving deep
into Mystery's enigmatic waters
is realizing who we truly are, even possible?

Patience and perseverance.
The Path reveals itself-
and the Work begins in earnest
after seemingly lifetimes,
those haunting moments
soaked in death, despair and aloneness,
dissolve.

Unclaimed parts of ourselves-
restlessly waiting in the wings,
longing to be noticed and valued-
stop looking outside
for satisfaction and love
and triumphantly, we step wholly on stage
to take our rightful place.

It's not talent that spurs one on to poetry
But
Rather
A desperate need to communicate something quickly
Especially to oneself

---J. Shima Moore 6/76 SF

The Last Call
by Cheryl

the Trumpet sounds,
Sun pulses---

My heartbeat skips--
I call for mercy.

I am a scribe,
recording these last times,
unsure of the next steps.

Perhaps, it matters not.
No future, No past--just Now,
and Now is OK.

Many thanks to these contributors:

Agatea
Cathleen Alexander
Molesley Bridgette (author of The Queen Code)
A'Marie B. Thomas-Brown
Elizabeth Carillo
Rune Darling
Trudie Giordano
Dave Harvey
Timothy Hershelman
Alex Hogstrum
Satarah Erikke Ingvild
Bodhi Holum Johnson
Natalya Koogler
Kazi Ayaz Mahesar
J Shima Moore
Pradeep Nawarathna (pcnawarathna@gmail.com)
Phillip Ortiz
Maya Rawitch
Susan Redwine
Janine Savient
Jane Seeley
Shambala
Shivrael
Daniel Stone
Mercy Talley
Cheryl Lunar Wind
Zarah Chelsie Nicole Wolivar
Le'Vell Zimmerman

Author page--

Cheryl Lunar Wind lives in the Mount Shasta area in a little town called Weed. She is a practicer of Mayan cosmology, Lakota ceremony, Star Knowledge and the Universal Laws including the Law of One. Her hobbies are writing poetry, music, dance, drum circles and love for all life; plant, animal and crystal. Cheryl has been a guide and spiritual teacher for many years. Now she shares wit and wisdom through poetry, and has published poetry books; Know Your Way, We Are One, Follow the White Rabbit, Love Your Light, LIFE: Shared thru Poetry, Come to Mount Shasta: Sacred Path Poetry, We Are Light, Finding Our Way Home, We Are Forever, Handshake With the Divine, Grand Rising: A New Day Has Dawned, Star Messages: Codes to Sing, Dance and Live by, Return to Innocence, Bloom Like Nature: Live the Natural Way, Creativity Brings Peace: Create & Share Your Gifts, May Love Lead, The Eventful Flash: Bringing Solar Waves of Change, The Setting Sun, Crossroads of Change, Step Into New Earth, Blessings Beyond Belief -- I Am: We Are, I Love Life and Life Loves Me, Love & Loss and now Ascension Flight 999: The Last Call.

Testimonials---

"Cheryl's poetry is very inspiring--particularly the way she compares life with the forces of nature. There is a special element in her poems that opens my heart and fills my soul with divine possiblities."
Giovanna Taormina, Co-Founder, One Circle Foundation

"Cheryl's poems have helped me to uncover and honor my own hidden memories. The beauty of her spirit is evident in each tender, insightful passage."
Marguerite Lorimer, www.earthalive.com

"A rare collection filled with raw, courageous honesty. Thought provoking words that will stop you in your tracks."
Snow Thorner, ED Open Sky Gallery, Montague, California

"When wisdom, guidance, confirming comfort, ect. arrives to us humans--from beings with the perspective of other realms--it is a divine gift. Especially in the form of what we call poetry, and through a being with no agenda; Cheryl Lunar Wind simply shares what source gives her!"---Dragon Love (Thomas) Budde

9 7 9 8 9 9 9 8 8 9 7 1 3 9